Ready-to-Go
Management Kit
for Teaching Genre

**by Debbie Deem, LuAnn Feely, Cheryl Fullmer,
Debbie Lienemann, and Katie Moore**

SCHOLASTIC
PROFESSIONALBOOKS

New York • Toronto • London • Auckland • Sydney
Mexico City • New Delhi • Hong Kong • Buenos Aires

Dedication

We would like to dedicate
this book to our families and friends
for supporting us throughout our
master's program and the
publication of this book.

We would like to thank
José Ribeiro for encouraging
us to pursue this project
for publication.

Cover design by Jorge Namerow
Cover artwork by Leanne Franson
Interior artwork by Mike Moran
Interior design by Sydney Wright

ISBN: 0-439-30360-5
Copyright © 2002 by Debbie Deem, LuAnn Feely, Cheryl Fullmer, Debbie Lienemann, Katie Moore
All rights reserved. Published by Scholastic Inc.
Printed in the U.S.A.

1 2 3 4 5 6 7 8 9 10   40   09 08 07 06 05 04 03 02

Contents

Introduction

Welcome to *Ready-to-Go Management Kit for Teaching Genre*! As you know, many students have read different genres and don't even realize it. On trips to the library, bookstore, or bookshelf, children may have even made decisions about their favorite kind of literature, types of characters, time periods, settings, and so on.

The activities in this book have been created to build on that knowledge. They are especially designed to help students gain skills in the area of critical reading. To that end, you'll find effective activities and resources that make the process of teaching genre more manageable, and the learning of genre even more enjoyable for kids.

We think you'll find that teaching genre has never been easier . . . or more fun!

How to Use This Book

Inside this book you'll find teacher-directed activities, student reproducibles, graphic organizers that can be used with any genre, classroom reproducibles, and a book list to help give students the support they need as they explore the characteristics of 10 genres.

Teacher-Directed Activities

Genre Profile

This is a brief summary of the most common characteristics of the genre. Turn to each boxed profile as you develop lesson plans and guide class discussions.

Have the class create genre posters. It's a fun, visual way to introduce the different genres. Provide students with a large piece of oaktag for each genre. Ask them to title each poster with the name of the genre, write a list of characteristics, and add drawings that help show how this genre is unique. Be sure to provide colorful markers and crayons for children to use as they decorate the posters. Each poster will be packed with information kids need. Hang them up and enjoy them all year long!

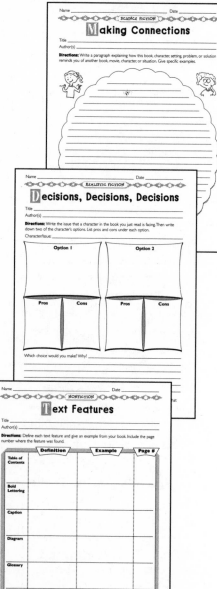

Pre-Reading Activities

These activities are intended to spark student interest in the genre. They work especially well for introducing the whole class to a particular genre, but can also be done in small groups, with partners, or individually.

During-Reading Activities

These activities are designed to strengthen the connections students make between the books they're reading and the genre characteristics they're learning to identify. The activities have been designed for students to do as a class or independently. They can also be done as a whole class, in small groups, or with partners.

After-Reading Activities

These activities help students think about what they've read and apply what they are learning about the characteristics of genre and story elements. They can be done in small groups, with partners, or individually.

Student Reproducibles

Packed with learning-filled activities young readers will love, these reproducibles give students practice with a variety of skills, including:

* identifying attributes of genres and related story elements;

* sequencing the action from beginning to end;

* explaining causes and effects of key plot points;

* summarizing a story, describing its big ideas.

6

Graphic Organizers for Teaching Any Genre

The graphic organizers on pages 92–94 can be used to introduce lessons on key topic areas, as follows:

* Story Map template—Students identify a book's genre and literary elements.

* Compare and Contrast template—Children categorize similarities and differences between genres, books, characters, settings, and so on.

* Cause and Effect template—Students identify key events within a book's plot and describe each event's origins and repercussions.

However you decide to use graphic organizers in the classroom, you're sure to find that they are helpful tools. Here are some ideas to get you started:

* Photocopy them and give them to students as class work or homework.

* Use them on your overhead projector. Just photocopy them onto transparency film and you're ready to go.

* Copy the organizer onto a dry-erase board or chalkboard. Then fill in and discuss the information as a class.

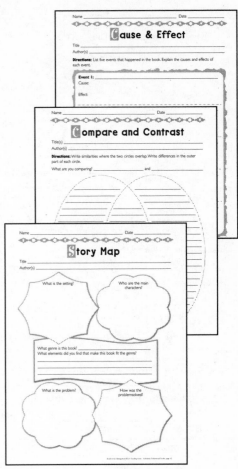

Classroom Reproducibles

We've included classroom reproducibles that can be photocopied, hole-punched, and placed in a binder for quick reference throughout the school year.

Genre Match

Use Genre Match on page 96 to determine how well students know what characteristics make

each genre unique. Consider having children complete the page in the fall as a baseline assessment and then periodically during the year to check their progress.

Student Reading Profile

Use the Student Reading Profile on page 97 to keep track of what books and genres children are reading. Whether you have students self-select books or you assign them specific books, this page is a handy way to stay organized.

Genre Study Record Keeper

To help make lesson planning a snap and to help you maintain a record of every student's progress, we've included the Genre Study Record Keeper on page 98. Just check off student reproducibles as each child completes them.

Book Links

You can use all of the teacher-directed activities and student reproducibles with any book! So, to make the search for learning-filled, age-appropriate books easier, we've included Book Links on page 103, a list of children's books that lend themselves to the study of each genre. The books on the list are great for addressing the specific needs of students with different reading levels and interests. They can be used for class read-alouds, and shared, paired, or independent reading.

Fun Activities for Every Learner

Here are some engaging activities that will help every student deepen comprehension and apply what he or she is learning about genre. Have children:

* examine a book's cover illustration and predict what might happen in the story;

* draw what happened during major events in the story;

* act out a section of a story or dress as a favorite character;

* retell the story to a classmate, friend, or family member.

Links to the Language Arts Standards

The National Council of Teachers of English (NCTE) and the International Reading Association (IRA) have collaborated and proposed what K–12 teachers should provide for their students to grow proficient in language arts. The reading and writing activities in this book support these standards and help students to:

* read a wide range of print and non-print texts to acquire new information;

* read a wide range of literature from many periods in many genres;

* apply a wide range of strategies to comprehend, interpret, evaluate, and appreciate texts;

* adjust their use of written and visual language to communicate effectively with a variety of audiences and for different purposes;

* employ a wide range of strategies as they write and use different writing process elements appropriately to communicate with different audiences for a variety of purposes;

* apply knowledge of language structure, language conventions, media techniques, figurative language, and genre to create, critique, and discuss print and non-print texts;

* use written and visual language to accomplish their own purposes.

These standards have been adapted from the NCTE and IRA Web sites: http://www.ncte.org and http://www.reading.org

Ready-to-Go Management Kit for Teaching Genre Scholastic Professional Books

Biography/ Autobiography

CHARACTERISTICS OF BIOGRAPHY

* Tells about a real person, past or present

* Is based on factual information

* Includes major influences (people, places, and events)

* Recounts key incidents in the person's life

CHARACTERISTICS OF AUTOBIOGRAPHY

* The main character is the author

* The author reveals feelings, reactions, and goals about events in his or her life

PRE-READING ACTIVITIES

Complete a few of the following activities as a class:

@ Brainstorm. Ask: *What makes the lives of certain people interesting to you?*

@ Examine the words *biography* and *autobiography*, breaking them into their root words (bio=life, graph=write, auto=self).

@ List elements of biography/autobiography in a web graphic organizer on the overhead. Apply each characteristic to someone the class is familiar with and write details under the appropriate headings.

@ Locate books of this genre in the library.

@ Make a class time line on adding-machine tape.

Ready-to-Go Management Kit for Teaching Genre Scholastic Professional Books

DURING-READING ACTIVITIES

Invite students to try a few of the following activities on their own:

* Read a biography or autobiography. List the book's characteristics that help classify it as a particular genre.

* Create a list of historical facts.

* Compare themselves with a character using both physical and character traits. Or, compare an autobiography to a biography about the same person.

* Draw a story map, complete with pictures that depict major influences in their life (people, places, events).

AFTER-READING ACTIVITIES

Have students try a few of the following activities on their own, with a partner, or in small groups:

* Draw a silhouette of the character. Underneath the silhouette, ask students to write important facts such as the person's name and date of birth.

* Make a list of questions to ask the character. Ask students to write the reason why each of those particular questions might elicit interesting information.

* Design a personal symbol. Using crayons or colored pencils, have students create a symbol or set of symbols that represent something that the person believed in or that reflects his or her life.

* Write a letter to the person. Have students first choose at least two major events from the character's life, then write about how they feel about what the person did, how he or she reacted, and why this was an important event. In the last part of the letter, have children do one or two of the following:

  • Describe something they have done that was similar in some way to what the person did.
  • Give encouragement or praise to the person.
  • Tell the person what he or she might have done if he or she had lived today.
  • Send the letter if the person is still alive.

* Create a portrait display. Ask each student to create a portrait of his or her famous person, adding the name and date of birth and date of death (if applicable). Have each student share with the class what he or she knows about the character.

Ready-to-Go Management Kit for Teaching Genre Scholastic Professional Books

Name _____   Date _____

Characteristics Web

Title _____

Author(s) _____

Directions: While reading, list information from the story under the appropriate category. Be sure to have at least two items of information under each category.

Tells about a real person

1

2

Includes major influences: people, places, and events

1

2

Is based on facts

1

2

Recounts key incidents in life

1

2

The author reveals feelings, reactions, or goals.

1

2

Name _____ Date _____

BIOGRAPHY / AUTOBIOGRAPHY

Events Catalog

Title _____

Author(s) _____

Directions: Keep a list of the important events in the person's life as they happen. Describe what happened, where it happened, who was involved, and how the person felt.

Event # l

What happened? _____

Where? _____

Who was involved with the person? Was he or she a help or hindrance?

_____

How did he or she feel? _____

Event #2

What happened? _____

Where? _____

Who was involved with the person? Was he or she a help or hindrance?

_____

How did he or she feel? _____

Event #3

What happened? _____

Where? _____

Who was involved with the person? Was he or she a help or hindrance?

_____

How did he or she feel? _____

What big event happened in your life that influenced you?

_____

_____

Where? _____

Who was involved with you to help you? Hinder you?

_____

How did you feel? _____

Name _____ Date _____

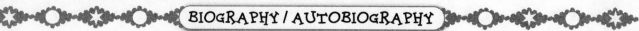

icture Map

Title _____

Author(s) _____

Directions: As you read, fill in the page using pictures, phrases, and words about the person whose life you are reading about.

Name _____ Date _____

Role Models

Title _____

Author(s) _____

Directions: In the top box, fill in the name of the person you are reading about and write a sentence stating whether or not the person is a good role model for others. In the bottom left box, list the qualities that add to his or her ability to be a role model, for example honesty or courage. In the bottom right box, give specific examples using short sentences from the book. Be sure to give the page numbers where the qualities can be found.

Was _____ a good role model for others?

_____

_____

_____

Qualities
_____

Proof
(Be sure to use details from the book.)
_____

1.

2.

3.

4.

5.

6.

Name _____ Date _____

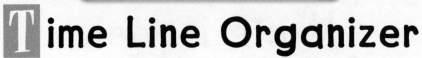Time Line Organizer

Title _____

Author(s) _____

Directions: On the left-hand side, keep a list of the important events in the person's life as they happened. Write one or two sentences to describe each event, or draw a picture to illustrate the event. On the right-hand side, list the date and place of each event in the story.

Event	Date/Place

Name _____ Date _____

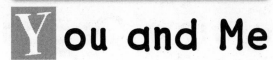 You and Me

Title _____

Author(s) _____

Directions: Compare and contrast the main character's life with your life. Write similarities where the two shapes overlap. Write differences in the outer part of each shape.

different

same

different

Name _____   Date _____

Interview Organizer

Title _____

Author(s) _____

Directions: Write six questions that you would like to ask the person you have read about. Include the person's answers and the character qualities they reveal.

Questions	Answers	Character Qualities
1. How did you feel when you chopped down the cherry tree?	I felt guilty.	very honest has integrity

Fairy Tales

CHARACTERISTICS OF FAIRY TALES

* Take place long ago. May begin with the phrase "once upon a time." May end with the phrase "lived happily ever after"

* Include magical characters, events, or places

* Share a lesson or moral for the reader to learn

* Contain characters who are either "good" or "bad"

* Features the numbers three or seven

* Are available in different versions because of their oral story-telling origins

PRE-READING ACTIVITIES

Complete a few of the following activities as a class:

@ As on ongoing activity throughout the study, display a map and mark where each fairy tale came from.

@ Have the students talk about their favorite fairy tales and why they like them.

@ Put a letter from a character (which you would need to create) on each student's desk. Have the letter ask the reader what the character should do about a problem in the tale. Ask students to write a response letter using any prior knowledge of the

Ready-to-Go Management Kit for Teaching Genre Scholastic Professional Books

fairy tale. Then read the tale together and discuss the answers they gave and how they compared with the story.

DURING-READING ACTIVITIES

Try a few of the following activities as a class:

* Read a fairy tale aloud. On chart paper, record events that are imaginary and events that are real.

* While reading aloud a fairy tale, have students raise their hand each time they hear one of the fairy tale characteristics. Discuss them briefly.

* Read more than one version of the same fairy tale. Then have a class discussion about similarities and differences.

* Create a chart that spotlights character qualities and physical traits.

AFTER-READING ACTIVITIES

Have students try a few of the following activities on their own, with a partner, or in small groups:

* Compare character qualities of two characters in different fairy tales using the graphic organizer on page 93.

* Perform a fairy tale as a Reader's Theater.

* Depict the setting of a fairy tale with crayons, markers, or tempera paint.

* Write a new ending to a fairy tale or rewrite it from the villain's point of view, developing a fractured fairy tale.

* Create fairy tales, applying what they know about the characteristics of the genre.

* Write a story that answers this question: *If you could have some kind of magic, what would it be and how would you use it?*

Ready-to-Go Management Kit for Teaching Genre Scholastic Professional Books

Name _____ Date _____

Letter to a Character

Title _____

Author(s) _____

Directions: Pretend you are one of the characters in a fairy tale you've read. Use this page to brainstorm three questions you would like to ask another character in the story. Then write a letter to that character asking the questions. Tell the character why you like or dislike him or her. Illustrate the border of your letter.

1. _____

_____

2. _____

_____

3. _____

_____

Name _____ Date _____

Fairy Tale Comparison Chart

Title _____ Title _____

Author(s) _____ Author(s) _____

Directions: After reading two versions of the same fairy tale, fill in the chart below. List all the things that are the same in both books in the "same" column. List all the things that are different in the "different" column.

Same	Different

Which version did you like best? Why? _____

_____

_____

Name _____ Date _____

Fairy Tale Lesson

Title _____

Author(s) _____

Directions: Use complete sentences to answer the questions below.

What is the lesson in the fairy tale you just read? _____

_____

_____

_____

_____

_____

_____

_____

_____

_____

_____

_____

Why is this an important lesson? _____

_____

_____

_____

_____

_____

_____

_____

_____

_____

_____

_____

Name _____ Date _____

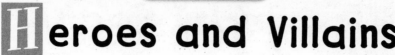

Title _____

Author(s) _____

Directions: Fill in the names of the heroes and villains for the fairy tales you read. Write two words describing each character.

Fairy Tales	Heroes	Villains

Name _____   Date _____

Popularity Graph

Title _____

Author(s) _____

Directions: In the space provided, write the titles of five well-known fairy tales. Ask at least 15 people which fairy tale is their favorite. Make tally marks to keep track, then use your data to complete the bar graph.

Titles	Tallies
1.	
2.	
3.	
4.	
5.	

_____
(graph title)

How many students picked the fairy tale as their favorite?

15					
14					
13					
12					
11					
10					
9					
8					
7					
6					
5					
4					
3					
2					
1					

1. (title)   2. (title)   3. (title)   4. (title)   5. (title)

Fairy Tales

Name _____   Date _____

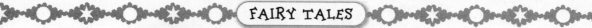

FAIRY TALES

Wanted Poster

Title _____

Author(s) _____

Directions: Draw a picture of the villain in your fairy tale and write a short paragraph that describes what the character is "wanted" for and why.

WANTED

_____
(Name)

_____

_____

_____

_____

_____

_____

Name _____ Date _____

Newspaper Article

Title _____

Author(s) _____

Directions: Use this page to help you write a newspaper article about a fairy tale as if the story takes place in the present time. Write your article on the back of the page. Include an illustration.

Who? _____

_____
_____
_____
_____
_____

What? _____

_____
_____
_____
_____

When? _____

_____
_____
_____
_____
_____
_____
_____
_____

Where? _____

_____
_____
_____
_____

Why? _____

_____
_____
_____
_____
_____

How? _____

_____
_____
_____
_____

Fantasy

CHARACTERISTICS OF FANTASY

* Major events cannot really happen

* Characters solve problems by using magic or other impossible strategies

* Contains elements that are not realistic

* Specific types: literary, quest, time travel, animal, miniature world, magic

PRE-READING ACTIVITIES

Complete a few of the following activities as a class:

@ Brainstorm a list of fantasy stories that students have read or seen in the movies. Ask: *Why can we categorize these stories as fantasy?*

@ Discuss how fantasy stories are different from other genres.

@ Write a list of words associated with the term *fantasy*.

@ Read a selection from a fantasy story that describes the setting. Have each student illustrate the setting with crayons or markers.

@ Introduce students to the specific types of fantasy stories:

  • Literary tales possess a style similar to traditional folklore.

Ready-to-Go Management Kit for Teaching Genre Scholastic Professional Books

- Quest stories contain battles between good and evil and struggles to overcome obstacles.

- Time travel stories allow characters to move freely between the present and other times and places.

- Animal stories feature animal characters with human abilities, such as talking, feeling, and thinking.

- Miniature world stories include miniature characters and settings.

- Magic stories contain problems that are solved in unexplainable ways.

DURING-READING ACTIVITIES

Try a one of the following activities as a class:

* Select a fantasy story to read aloud. Then have the class predict what will happen. During the reading, have students confirm or deny their predictions and make new predictions.

* Discuss the character and traits used to describe the character. Invite students to give examples from the story to support their opinions. Then create a class chart of character traits.

AFTER-READING ACTIVITIES

Have students try one of the following activities on their own, with a partner, or in small groups:

* Pretend to be a character from the fantasy story. Discuss how your lives are similar and different.

* Make a list of the events from the story that could really happen and the events that could not really happen.

Name _____ Date _____

Identifying Story Elements

Title _____

Author(s) _____

Directions: Write two or three sentences describing the fantasy story elements found in the book that you read. Be sure to give specific examples.

Major events cannot really happen:

_____

_____

_____

_____

_____

_____

Characters solve problems using magic or other impossible strategies:

_____

_____

_____

_____

_____

_____

_____

Contains elements that are not realistic:

_____

_____

_____

_____

_____

_____

Name _____ Date _____

Types of Fantasy

Title _____

Author(s) _____

Types of fantasy include:

Literary—a style similar to traditional folklore

Quest—contains battles between good and evil and struggles to overcome obstacles

Time travel—characters move freely between the present and other times and places

Animal—animal characters have human abilities, such as talking, feeling, and thinking

Miniature world—includes miniature characters and settings

Magic—problems are solved in unexplainable ways

Directions: Using complete sentences, explain which fantasy type best describes the book you have read. Be sure to give specific examples and page numbers from the book to support your answer.

This book represents an example of _____ fantasy.

_____

_____

_____

_____

_____

_____

_____

_____

_____

_____

_____

Name _____ Date _____

Problem & Solution

Title _____

Author(s) _____

Directions: Describe the problem and solution in the book you have read. Be sure to give specific examples.

What was the problem?
Did the characters use magic or other
impossible solutions to help them solve it?

_____

_____

_____

_____

_____

_____

_____

_____

_____

Could the problems have been solved using a realistic solution? How?

_____

_____

_____

_____

_____

_____

_____

_____

Name _____ Date _____

Illustrate a Character

Title _____

Author(s) _____

Directions: Choose a favorite fantasy character and draw an illustration of him or her. Be sure to include specific details that make this character memorable.

What is the character's name? _____

Why did you choose to illustrate this character? _____

_____

_____

_____

Name _____ Date _____

What Happened When?

Title _____

Author(s) _____

Directions: Describe five important events in the story. List them in the order that they took place.

Events

1.

2.

3.

4.

5.

Name _____ Date _____

 FANTASY

Character Paragraphs

Title _____

Author(s) _____

Directions: Recall the most difficult problem in your fantasy book.

In your own words, tell how the main character dealt with this problem. What did you learn about the main character from how he or she solved the problem?

_____

_____

_____

_____

_____

_____

★··★

List the qualities that the main character showed during this difficult time. Write about why you admire or do not admire these qualities.

_____

_____

_____

_____

_____

★··★

What problem-solving abilities do you have? Write about a time when you solved a problem using your strengths.

_____

_____

_____

_____

_____

_____

Name _____ Date _____

Title _____

Author(s) _____

Directions: List at least five movies, TV shows, or commercials that you have seen which contain fantasy elements. Describe the fantasy elements.

Name of Movie, TV show, or Commercial	Fantasy Elements

Historical Fiction

CHARACTERISTICS OF HISTORICAL FICTION

* Contains historical accuracy

* Takes place in the past

* Includes language that represents the time and place

* Includes illustrations that are historically accurate

PRE-READING ACTIVITIES

Complete a few of the following activities as a class:

* Ask students to point out any new or unfamiliar vocabulary.

* Share a video or audiotape that introduces students to the dialect of the region.

* Discuss the characteristics of historical fiction.

* Invite students to tell the names of stories or movies they've read that fall into the genre of historical fiction.

DURING-READING ACTIVITIES

Invite students to try a few of the following activities on their own:

* Make a class time line of the historical events.

* Create a characteristic map of the main character.

* Keep a list of unfamiliar words.

Ready-to-Go Management Kit for Teaching Genre Scholastic Professional Books

* Paint a picture detailing one of the settings in the historical fiction book.

AFTER-READING ACTIVITIES

Have students try a few of the following activities on their own, with a partner, or in small groups:

* Create a time capsule showing their understanding of the time period.

* Plan a time-period party.

* Design a travel brochure that promotes the setting of the historical fiction book.

* Using an opinion proof format, decide if the main historical event in the historical fiction book impacted people in a positive or negative way.

* Prove that the book they read is historical fiction by creating a storyboard. On a piece of construction paper draw pictures that illustrate the book. Capture all of the characteristics of historical fiction: historical accuracy, the setting (the past), and language that represents the time and place.

* Conduct a talk-show interview.

* Write an epitaph.

Name _____   Date _____

Character Map

Title _____

Author(s) _____

Directions: Complete the following chart for the main character of the book you read. Write the title, author, and main character in the middle shape. Now think of four characteristics or traits of this character. Write those in the oval shapes. For each trait, think of two times in the book when the character displayed this trait. Write these examples in the rectangles.

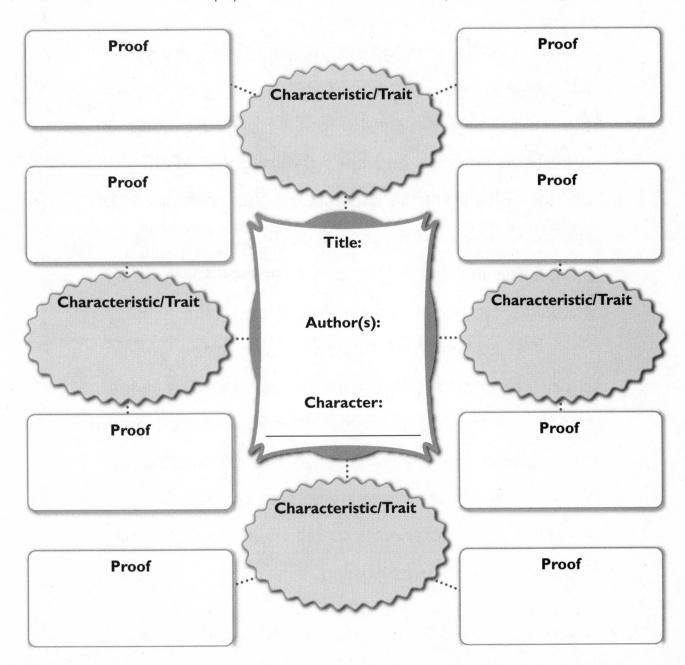

Proof

Proof

Characteristic/Trait

Proof

Proof

Characteristic/Trait

Title:

Author(s):

Character:

_____

Characteristic/Trait

Proof

Proof

Characteristic/Trait

Proof

Proof

Name _____ Date _____

Could This Be True?

Title _____

Author(s) _____

Directions: Read the following excerpt. Highlight all of the parts that could not have possibly happened during that time period.

It was a cold winter day in the year 1868. Pa had just come in the front door after working all day in the field. You could smell a loaf of bread baking in the bread machine and hear the laughter of the children playing in the other room. Ma greeted Pa at the door with a warm cup of coffee and had him sit in his chair in front of the gas fireplace to warm up. Pa asked Ma to turn on the television to the evening news to find out what was happening in the world. Ma abided and set the table for supper. She lit the candles on the tables as the UPS man knocked on the door with a delivery. Pa opened the package and found a brand-new computer. After supper, Pa e-mailed all of his friends to tell them about the big winter storm that was coming.

Name _____ Date _____

The Life and Times of...

_____

Title _____

Author(s) _____

Directions: Add details to each topic for the character you just read about. Include at least three details for each topic.

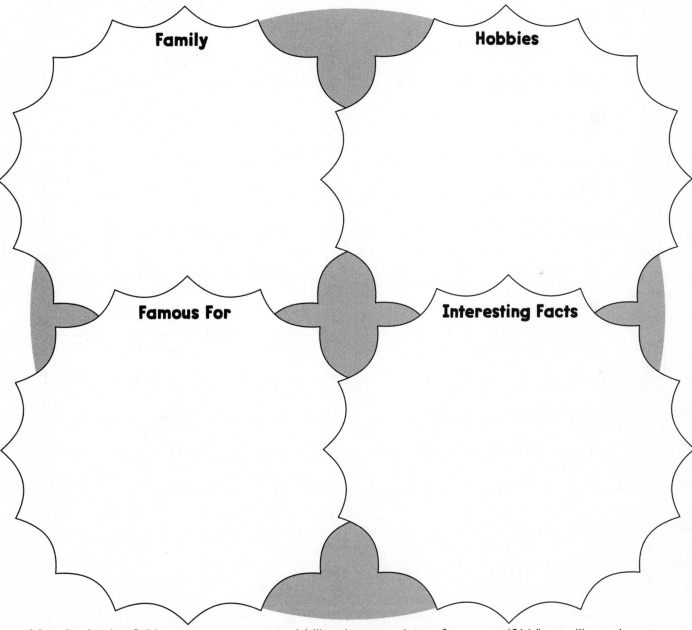

Family

Hobbies

Famous For

Interesting Facts

Use the back of this page to create a grid like the one above for yourself! What will you be famous for in the future?

Name _____ Date _____

ho, What, When, Where, Why, How?

Title _____

Author(s) _____

Directions: Use this worksheet to take notes on the historical fiction book you just read. You will use these notes to write a newspaper article on the *Extra! Extra!* page.

WHO?	**WHAT?**
_____	_____
_____	_____
_____	_____
_____	_____
_____	_____
_____	_____
WHEN?	**WHERE?**
_____	_____
_____	_____
_____	_____
_____	_____
WHY?	**HOW?**
_____	_____
_____	_____
_____	_____
_____	_____
_____	_____

Name _____ Date _____

Extra! Extra!

Title _____

Author(s) _____

Directions: Use the answers that you wrote on your *Who, What, When, Where, Why, How?* worksheet to write a newspaper article describing the historical event that occurred in the book.

Name _____ Date _____

otes About a Main Character

Title _____

Author(s) _____

Directions: Use this sheet to record information about a main character in the book you just read.

Facts	Details
Birth/death: (dates and locations)	
Place lived:	
Family:	
Personality:	
Other interesting facts:	

Name _____ Date _____

pitaph

Title _____

Author(s) _____

Choose one character from the book you just read and imagine that character has died. On the tombstone below, write the epitaph that would be carved on it. Epitaphs tell important information about a person in just a few sentences.

Nonfiction

CHARACTERISTICS OF NONFICTION

* Focuses on specific subjects or controlling ideas

* Is supported by facts

* Organizes facts; has text features such as table of contents, index, and glossary

* Uses examples and explanations to clarify ideas

* Includes realistic illustrations or photographs

PRE-READING ACTIVITIES

Complete a few of the following activities as a class:

@ Share a literary example along with a fact-driven nonfiction book and compare and contrast the two. (See wolf books suggested on page 107.)

@ Discuss ways in which nonfiction starts: with a statement, description, or fact. (See suggested book, *Bold and Bright Black-and-White Animals*.)

@ Point out text features of nonfiction books (table of contents, bold lettering, captions, diagrams, index, and glossary) and tell how to locate and use each feature.

@ Develop a coding system to mark information in the books using sticky notes. For example, a star could indicate an interesting fact and a question mark could indicate a question.

Ready-to-Go Management Kit for Teaching Genre Scholastic Professional Books

- Brainstorm nonfiction topics that interest your students and choose one to explore as a class.

- Have a scavenger hunt for text features. Have each student (or partners) go to the library and pick a nonfiction book. Ask them to look for the text features and record page numbers and examples using the reproducible on page 48.

DURING-READING ACTIVITIES

Invite students to try one of the following activities on their own:

* Make a list of questions they think of while reading. As they locate the answers to their questions, have them record them.

* Survey their classmates to see if anyone has background knowledge about their topic. Then invite students to interview their peers.

AFTER-READING ACTIVITIES

Have students try a few of the following activities on their own, with a partner, or in small groups:

* List three new facts that they learned from reading the selection.

* Encourage students to check other sources on the same topic for further information. Then have them pair up and share their new information with each other.

* Use facts to write a fictional story.

Name _____ Date _____

Text Features

Title _____

Author(s) _____

Directions: Define each text feature and give an example from your book. Include the page number where the feature was found.

	Definition	Example	Page #
Table of Contents			
Bold Lettering			
Caption			
Diagram			
Glossary			
Index			

Name _____ Date _____

Nonfiction Versus Fiction

Directions: Find a nonfiction book and a fiction book about the same topic, such as a bear. Read each book, then list the characteristics that make one a nonfiction book and the other a fiction book. Remember to list the title and author(s) of each book.

Common topic: _____

_____

_____

_____

_____

NONFICTION (true)

Title: _____

Author(s): _____

Characteristics: _____

_____

_____

_____

_____

_____

FICTION (not true)

Title: _____

Author(s): _____

Characteristics: _____

_____

_____

_____

_____

_____

Name _____   Date _____

What's It All About?

Title _____

Author(s) _____

Directions: After reading a nonfiction book, write the five most important facts that the book told about on the lines below. Use complete sentences.

Most important facts from this book:

1. _____

_____

2. _____

_____

3. _____

_____

4. _____

_____

5. _____

_____

Use these important facts to write a brief summary of the book.

_____

_____

_____

_____

_____

_____

_____

_____

_____

Name _____ Date _____

Question the Topic

Topic _____

Directions: In the first column, write five questions about a topic of your choice. Then search nonfiction books to find the answers. Write them down in the second column. In the third column write the title of the book(s) that helped answer each question. Then, in the final column list the text feature(s) that helped you locate the answers.

Question:	Answer:	Title of Book(s):	Feature(s):
1.			
2.			
3.			
4.			
5.			

Name _____ Date _____

KWL

Title _____

Author(s) _____

Topic _____

Directions: Before reading a nonfiction book, fill in the first two columns. After reading the book, complete the third column. Circle items that were correct from columns one and two after you read.

Before Reading: What I Think I KNOW	Before Reading: What I WONDER	After Reading: What I LEARNED

Name _____ Date _____

Table of Facts

Title _____

Author(s) _____

Directions: Using knowledge that you learned from reading, create a table, chart, or diagram to share information from your book. Remember to label all parts and to give your table, chart, or diagram a title.

For example, if you read about bears you could:

• create a diagram of a bear's body parts;

• create a chart listing interesting statistics about the bear;

• create a table comparing different types of bears.

Name _____ Date _____

Captions

Directions: Look in magazines to find a picture that you find interesting. Trim the picture and paste it below. Then write a creative and fact-filled caption about the picture.

You may need to reference some nonfiction books to find out about the picture and/or how to write a caption. If you use a nonfiction book, include the title and author.

Title _____

Author(s) _____

Poetry

> **CHARACTERISTICS OF POETRY** ·············· ✳
> * Is written to bring out emotions and feelings
> * Often uses rhythm and rhyme
> * Plays with language
> * There are many different types

PRE-READING ACTIVITIES

Complete a few of the following activities as a class:

* Read aloud two different types of poems (such as "Lazy Jane" by Shel Silverstein, and "Pencil and Paint" by Eleanor Farjeon). Ask students to discuss what they just heard. Compare how the poems are alike and different. Write the ideas on the chalkboard. Help students notice the tones, rhythms, patterns, and purposes.

* Invite students to tell about poems they've enjoyed, the first poem they remember hearing or reading, and the poems they use during games.

* Talk with students about feelings evoked by poems. Ask: *How do poems make you feel inside?* Make a list on chart paper to display in the classroom.

DURING-READING ACTIVITIES ·······················✳

Try a few of the following activities as a class:

* Read aloud a poem that creates a visual picture in the reader's mind (such as "The Paper Bag" by Zaro Weil). Have students close their eyes and visualize as you read. Then have them draw a picture of what they saw.

Ready-to-Go Management Kit for Teaching Genre Scholastic Professional Books

* Read three poems with different rhyming patterns (such as "The President" by Dee Anderson, "How Do You Like to Go Up in a Swing" by Robert Louis Stevenson, and "New Kid" by Mike Makley). Encourage students to discover each pattern and then to find more on their own.

* Read aloud a poem that uses two different voices (such as "Peter Ping and Patrick Pong" by Dennis Lee) to help illustrate how language play is used in poetry. Have two students act out the poem for the class.

* Brainstorm a list of all the different subjects covered in the poems you have been reading. Use this to show students that poems can be written about anything.

* Read aloud a poem to introduce repetition (such as "Time" by Mary Ann Hoberman).

* Introduce the concept of alliteration with a poem (such as "Friendly Frederick Fiddlestone" by Arnold Lobel).

* Write a class poem about school using a simple ABAB rhyme pattern.

* Have each student copy and illustrate his or her favorite poem on poster board. Display the posters in the hallway for other students to see.

* Have students memorize and recite a poem. Encourage the use of props, costumes, and actions.

AFTER-READING ACTIVITIES

Have students try one of the following activities on their own, with a partner, or in small groups:

* Read aloud a poem that demonstrates feelings (such as "When I Misbehave" by Eloise Greenfield). Have students write down the feelings they have after hearing the poem.

* Find a poem that paints a word picture by using various sizes, fonts, and formats (such as "Rolling Down a Hill" by Colin West). Have students work in partners to find other shape poems. Have each pair share their favorite shape poem with the class.

Ready-to-Go Management Kit for Teaching Genre Scholastic Professional Books

Name _____ Date _____

Feeling Poems

Directions: Find three different poems: one that makes you happy, one that makes you sad, and one that makes you curious. Then answer the questions below.

What is the title and author of the poem that made you feel happy?

Title _____

Author _____

Why did this poem make you feel happy?

List some of the words from the poem that made you feel happy

What is the title and author of the poem that made you feel sad?

Title _____

Author _____

Why did this poem make you feel sad?

List some of the words from the poem that made you feel sad.

What is the title and author of the poem that made you feel curious?

Title _____

Author _____

Why did this poem make you feel curious?

List some of the words from the poem that made you feel curious.

Name _____ Date _____

Haiku

Directions: Read several haiku poems and list their titles and authors here:

Title _____

Author(s) _____

Title _____

Author(s) _____

Title _____

Author(s) _____

What pattern do they follow? Notice the syllables in every line. An easy way to figure out how many syllables a word has is to feel how many times your chin drops when you say the word aloud.

_____

_____

_____

_____

_____

_____

_____

_____

_____

Remembering that most all haiku poems are about nature, write your own haiku poem.

_____

_____

_____

_____

_____

_____

_____

_____

Name _____ Date _____

Alliteration Adventure

Directions: Read several short poems that use alliteration (words that start with the same initial sound) and list their titles here:

Title _____

Author(s) _____

Title _____

Author(s) _____

Title _____

Author(s) _____

Now try writing your own alliterative poem. Underline the repeated sound each time it appears in your poem.

_____

_____

_____

_____

_____

_____

_____

_____

_____

_____

_____

_____

_____

_____

_____

_____

_____

_____

_____

Name _____ Date _____

POETRY

Write Your Own Poem

Directions: Choose any format and write your own poem about any topic. Be sure to edit your writing and illustrate your poem.

Format _____

Poem Title _____

_____

_____

_____

_____

_____

_____

_____

_____

_____

_____

Name _____ Date _____

POETRY

Letter to a Poet

Title _____

Author(s) _____

Directions: Use the stationery below to write an admiring letter to your favorite poet. Be sure to tell this poet about your favorite poem, and why you like his or her writing.

_____

_____

_____

Dear _____ ,

_____

_____

_____

_____

_____

_____

_____

_____

_____

_____

_____

_____

_____

_____

Sincerely,

_____

P.S. _____

Name _____ Date _____

Poet's Style

Directions: Read three poems written by the same poet. Record the poet and poems below. Write a list of elements or ideas you find in common within all three poems and give examples of each.

Poet _____

Poem _____

Poem _____

Poem _____

THINGS IN COMMON	EXAMPLES

In one sentence, what can you say about your poet's style? _____

_____

_____

_____

POETRY

Shape Poems

Directions: Find and read three shape poems. Record the titles and authors below. Then answer the questions in complete sentences.

1. Title _____

Author(s) _____

2. Title _____

Author(s) _____

3. Title _____

Author(s) _____

Questions:

1. Do the words of any of the poems have anything to do with the shape the author chose? Include examples from the poems.

_____

_____

_____

_____

2. Did the shapes of the poems help you understand the words better?

_____

_____

_____

_____

3. Why do you think authors choose to write shape poems?

_____

_____

_____

_____

Write your own shape poem on the back of this paper.

Realistic Fiction

CHARACTERISTICS OF REALISTIC FICTION

* Is set in a time and place that actually does exist or could exist

* Features characters that reflect people we know

* Includes a problem and resolution

* Contains fast-paced action that could really happen

PRE-READING ACTIVITIES

Complete a few of the following activities as a class:

@ Brainstorm a list of things that happen in everyday life.

@ Discuss ways in which the characteristics of realistic fiction differ from other kinds of fiction, such as historical fiction and fantasy.

@ Create a class list of places students have traveled. Take this a step further by putting up a world map and placing a thumbtack at each location.

Ready-to-Go Management Kit for Teaching Genre Scholastic Professional Books

DURING-READING ACTIVITIES ·············· ✱

Invite students to try a few of the following activities on their own:

* ✱ Select one sentence in the book and illustrate it using crayons, colored pencils, or markers.

* ✱ Keep track of the conflict in the book and what happens until it is resolved.

* ✱ Write about something that happened to them that was like something that happened to the character in the book.

AFTER-READING ACTIVITIES ·············· ✱

Have students try a few of the following activities on their own, with a partner, or in small groups:

* ✱ Create puppets of the main characters, using details from the book about hair color, clothing style, height, and facial features.

* ✱ Rewrite a key event in the story from another character's point of view.

* ✱ Write a letter to a favorite character in the story, explaining why he or she is unlike other characters.

* ✱ Depict an event in the story with cartoons. Then have a class discussion about the challenges of showing character qualities in a cartoon.

◆ 65 ◆

Name _____ Date _____

erspectives

Title _____

Author(s) _____

Directions: Very often when an event happens, those involved understand the event in different ways. Choose an event from your book and look at it from different characters' points of view. In the grid below, record the event and each character's perspective on it.

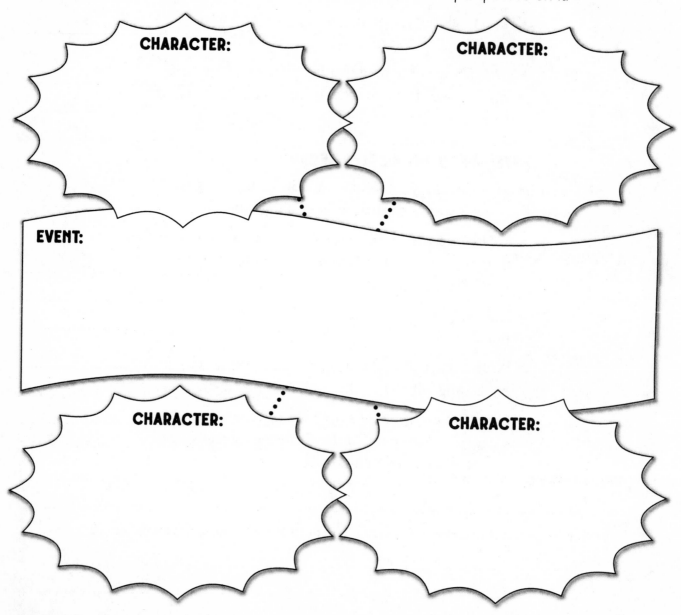

CHARACTER:

CHARACTER:

EVENT:

CHARACTER:

CHARACTER:

Extension: Think of an event from your life that really affected you. Describe the time with as much detail as possible taking care to show how you felt. When you are finished, try to step into another person's shoes and describe the event from his or her perspective.

Name _____ Date _____

Story Steps

Title _____

Author(s) _____

Directions: In most pieces of literature there is a conflict or problem. The problem does not arise quickly. There are usually a series of connected events that lead to the main conflict. Complete the following sentences about the main conflict in your story. Then answer the questions below.

Conflict: _____

First, _____

_____

_____

Then, _____

_____

_____

Then, _____

_____

_____

Now, _____

_____

_____

How was the problem solved? _____

_____

In order to avoid this problem, what else could the character(s) have done?

_____

_____

What would you have done? _____

_____

Name _____ Date _____

Telegram

Title _____

Author(s) _____

Directions: Summarize the book you just read using 50 words or less.

_____

_____

_____

_____

_____

_____

_____

Now work with a partner to write a telegram summary. You will need to reduce your 50-word summary to 30 words or less.

_____

_____

_____

_____

_____

_____

_____

_____

_____

_____

_____

Remember:
A telegram is a short message that is electronically transmitted and delivered in paper form. The sender is charged a fee for each word that is sent!

Write your partner's name here: _____

Name _____ Date _____

Decisions, Decisions, Decisions

Title _____

Author(s) _____

Directions: Write the issue that a character in the book you just read is facing. Then write down two of the character's options. List pros and cons under each option.

Character/Issue: _____

Option 1	**Option 2**

Pros	**Cons**	**Pros**	**Cons**

Which choice would you make? Why? _____

_____

_____

_____

_____

_____

On the back of this page, write about a difficult decision you made and why you chose what you did.

Name _____ Date _____

bstacles

Title _____

Author(s) _____

Directions: In life, everyone has obstacles to overcome. Some examples of obstacles can include physical challenges and emotional pain. These obstacles can be difficult to deal with, but they can be overcome.

1 What obstacle is the character facing?

2 How is the character dealing with this obstacle?

3 What advice would you give to the character as he or she tries to overcome this obstacle?

Name _____ Date _____

Lights, Camera, Action!

Title _____

Author(s) _____

Directions: Think of four main events that happened in the book you just read. Write down a short summary of each event, then list the characters and props that you would need to act out that event in a movie.

EVENTS	CHARACTERS	PROPS

Name _____ Date _____

Get a Job

Title _____

Author(s) _____

Directions: Complete the job application below for a character in the book you just read.

Name: _____

Address: _____

_____

Phone number: _____

Position applying for: _____

Why are you qualified for this job?

_____

_____

_____

_____

What past jobs have you had?

_____

_____

_____

_____

Why should we hire you?

_____

_____

_____

_____

Signature _____ Date _____

Now pretend you are interviewing for a job. What are you good at doing? Use the back of this page to explain.

Science Fiction

CHARACTERISTICS OF SCIENCE FICTION ·······*

* Major events might really happen in the near or distant future on Earth or another planet

* Characters solve problems using scientific data or technology

* Is based on scientific fact and futuristic technology

* Specific types: Mind control, Tomorrow's world, Survival

PRE-READING ACTIVITIES

Complete a few of the following activities as a class:

@ Introduce students to the specific types of science fiction stories:

  • Mind control stories contain a character whose mind is controlled by someone or something else
  • Tomorrow's world stories take place in the future
  • Survival tales describe how characters survive specific problems

DURING-READING ACTIVITIES

Invite students to try a few of the following activities on their own:

* Make a list of scientific facts from the story.

* Compare the characters to kids today.

* Imagine making a movie of the book. List locations that could be used for filming and state why those places reflect the setting in the book.

* List three or four sentences from the book that show what type of science fiction the story is.

AFTER-READING ACTIVITIES

Have students try a few of the following activities on their own, with a partner, or in small groups:

* Create a diorama to show the futuristic setting.

* Make a model of futuristic inventions using cardboard, papier mâché, clay, or foam. Label each part with its name and function.

* Write a description of the setting using vivid details, including: sights, sounds, smells, tastes, and the way objects feel when touched.

* Research the scientific technology or inventions that exist in the story. Write a report that answers these questions:

  • How would the invention or technology benefit people today?

  • If scientists are researching how to invent the technology, what progress have they made?

  • Do you think today's scientists will succeed in creating the technology from the book you read? Why or why not?

Ready-to-Go Management Kit for Teaching Genre Scholastic Professional Books

Name _____   Date _____

Time Capsule

Title _____

Author(s) _____

Directions: A time capsule is used to store items which represent a certain time period. Select five items that you might store in a time capsule to explain life today. Think of five items that the main character in your book might select to represent his or her time period. Be sure to explain why each item should be placed in the time capsule.

My Items	Character's Items (Name: _____)
1. _____	**1.** _____
Why? _____	**Why?** _____
_____	_____
_____	_____
2. _____	**2.** _____
Why? _____	**Why?** _____
_____	_____
_____	_____
3. _____	**3.** _____
Why? _____	**Why?** _____
_____	_____
_____	_____
4. _____	**4.** _____
Why? _____	**Why?** _____
_____	_____
_____	_____
5. _____	**5.** _____
Why? _____	**Why?** _____
_____	_____
_____	_____

Name _____ Date _____

Character Traits

Title _____

Author(s) _____

Directions: Write the name of the main character in the center shape. In the shapes that surround it, write and give examples of four traits to describe the character.

Trait

_____

Example

Trait

_____

Example

Name

_____

Trait

_____

Example

Trait

_____

Example

Name _____   Date _____

Making Connections

Title _____

Author(s) _____

Directions: Write a paragraph explaining how this book, character, setting, problem, or solution reminds you of another book, movie, character, or situation. Give specific examples.

Name _____ Date _____

One Hundred Years From Now

Title _____

Author(s) _____

Directions: Use this form to help you plan a news story happening one hundred years from now. Use your plan to create a newscast or newspaper article detailing the story.

Who?

What?

When?

Where?

Why?

How?

Write your article on the back of this page.

Name _____ Date _____

Science Fiction Story Elements

Title _____

Author(s) _____

Directions: Write two to three sentences describing the science fiction story elements found in the book that you read. Be sure to give specific examples from the book.

Major events that might really happen:

Characters solve problems using scientific data or technology:

Is based on scientific fact and futuristic technology:

Name _____ Date _____

Types of Science Fiction

Title _____

Author(s) _____

Directions: Explain which science fiction type best fits the book you have completed. Be sure to give specific examples and page numbers from the book to support your answer.

> Types of science fiction include:
>
> **Mind control**—a character's mind is controlled by someone or something else
>
> **Tomorrow's world**—story takes place in the future
>
> **Survival**—story describes how characters survive specific problems

This book represents an example of _____ science fiction.

Example	Page #

Name _____ Date _____

Same Problem, Different Solution

Title _____

Author(s) _____

Directions: Describe the problem and solution in your book. Did the character use scientific data or technology to help solve the problem?

_____

_____

_____

_____

_____

_____

_____

_____

_____

Write a paragraph describing another way the problem could be solved using scientific data or futuristic technology.

_____

_____

_____

_____

_____

_____

_____

_____

_____

_____

_____

Tall Tales

CHARACTERISTICS OF TALL TALES

✳ Consider using this acronym to help your students remember the characteristics that set tall tales apart from other kinds of fiction:

T is for the trickery or cleverness used by the main character.

A is for the main character's adventures in our country's westward expansion.

L is for larger-than-life qualities of the main character, who is usually based on a real person.

E is for the exaggeration used in the story to make it entertaining.

PRE-READING ACTIVITIES

Complete a few of the following activities as a class:

 Introduce the concept of exaggerations and their entertainment value during storytelling.

Introduce similes. Explain that a *simile* is a comparison of unlike things using the words *like* or *as*. (Example: His teeth are shiny like diamonds.)

Ready-to-Go Management Kit for Teaching Genre Scholastic Professional Books

@ Make two charts, one labeled "Physical Traits" the other labeled "Character Traits." Add examples from tall tales as they are read. Display the chart in the classroom for future reference.

@ Put up a map of the continental United States. Invite students to explain what they know about westward expansion. Then mark areas in which characters traveled. Keep the map up throughout the genre study and encourage students to add to it.

DURING-READING ACTIVITIES

Invite students to try a few of the following activities on their own:

* Create a time line for the main character in a tall tale.

* Select a sentence to visualize, then write it across the bottom of the page and illustrate it.

* Keep a list of all of the exaggerations they discover while reading.

AFTER-READING ACTIVITIES

Have students try a few of the following activities on their own, with a partner, or in small groups:

* Compare and contrast different versions of the same character or tale.

* Design a wanted poster for a character. Include the character's name and why he or she is wanted.

* Have students pretend they are the character and write a letter to their parents explaining their adventures in the order that they happened.

Ready-to-Go Management Kit for Teaching Genre Scholastic Professional Books

Name _____ Date _____

Exaggerations

Title _____

Author(s) _____

Directions: List the exaggerations from the story as you read them. Write in complete sentences. Then pick one exaggeration and explain how it contributed to the story.

Exaggeration: _____
_____
_____

Exaggeration: _____
_____
_____

Exaggeration: _____
_____
_____

Exaggeration: _____
_____
_____

Exaggeration: _____
_____
_____

Pick one exaggeration and explain how it contributed to the story.
_____
_____
_____
_____
_____
_____

Name _____ Date _____

Illustrate a Simile

Title _____

Author(s) _____

Directions: Select a simile that you would like to illustrate, and write it at the bottom of the page. Then illustrate the simile in the box below.

Simile: _____

I found the simile on page _____.

Name _____   Date _____

Real or Superhuman Character Traits

Title _____

Author(s) _____

Directions: As you read, make a list of character traits or physical traits that make the character seem real (such as honest, works hard). On the right side, list the character traits that make the character larger than life or superhuman. (For example: He can knock down 50 trees with one swing of an axe.)

Character: _____

REAL	SUPERHUMAN

Name _____ Date _____

Hero/Heroine?

Title _____

Author(s) _____

Directions: On the left side, write a sentence stating whether or not your character is a hero/heroine. On the right side, give specific examples to support your statement using short sentences from the book. Be sure to give the page numbers where the evidence can be found.

Was _____ a hero/heroine?

Opinion	**Proof** (details from the book)
	1.
	2.
	3.
	4.
	5.
	6.
	7.
	8.

Name _____ Date _____

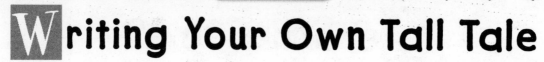

Writing Your Own Tall Tale

Title _____

Author(s) _____

Directions: Answer the following questions to organize your thoughts. Then use the back of this page to write your own tall tale.

WHO? Who do I already know that I can write about? (Example: My grandmother.)

_____

WHAT? What do I know about this person? (Example: She had blue eyes, short but strong legs, and was a hard worker.)

_____

WHEN? When did this person's adventures take place? (Example: Throughout the 1900s. She was born in 1910 and is still living.)

_____

WHERE? Where did the person's adventures take place? (Example: She was born in Alma, Nebraska, and now lives in Holdrege, Nebraska.)

_____

In what ways did this person use trickery? (Example: She always wore long-sleeved shirts to trick people so they would not know she had strong arms made of steel.)

1. _____

2. _____

What adventures did this person have? (Example: She was a teacher in a one-room school-house, worked in a department store, and finally worked on the farm with my grandfather.)

1. _____

2. _____

In what ways was this person larger than life? (Example: She was 5' 2" tall and weighed 98 pounds. Seventy pounds of her were her strong arms of steel.)

1. _____

2. _____

In what ways were this person's skills exaggerated? (Example: She would milk the cows with just one or two pulls because her arms were so strong.)

1. _____

2. _____

Name _____   Date _____

crostic Poem

Title _____

Author(s) _____

Directions: Write a poem about a character you've read about. Down the left side of the box, write that character's name. Next to each letter of the name, write a word or phrase that describes that character's physical or personality traits. Illustrate the border that surrounds the poem. For example:

          Big muscles
          Unmistakably strong
          Never quits
          Your friend
          Adventurous
          Navigated the frontier

Name _____ Date _____

Guess Who?

Title _____

Author(s) _____

Directions: In each shape, write clues about a character you've read about. Each clue should give a hint that tells about the character. For example: physical traits and hobbies.

On the back of this page, write the character's name. Then trade papers with a friend. Can your friend guess the character's name?

Graphic Organizers
to be Used With Any Book

Name _____ Date _____

Story Map

Title _____

Author(s) _____

What is the setting?

Who are the main characters?

What genre is this book? _____
What elements did you find that make this book fit the genre?

_____

_____

_____

What is the problem?

How was the problem solved?

Name _____ Date _____

Compare and Contrast

Title(s) _____

Author(s) _____

Directions: Write similarities where the two circles overlap. Write differences in the outer part of each circle.

What are you comparing? _____ and _____

same

different   **different**

Name _____ Date _____

Cause & Effect

Title _____

Author(s) _____

Directions: List five events that happened in the book. Explain the causes and effects of each event.

Event 1: _____

Cause:

Effect:

Event 2: _____

Cause:

Effect:

Event 3: _____

Cause:

Effect:

Event 4: _____

Cause:

Effect:

Event 5: _____

Cause:

Effect:

Classroom Resources

Name _____ Date _____

Genre Match

Directions: Ten genres are listed on the left. Find a match for each genre from the examples on the right. Write the letter next to the genre it matches.

GENRES	EXAMPLES
1 ____ Poetry	**A.** Two talking cats teach a mouse how to talk.
2 ____ Historical Fiction	**B.** There are nine planets in the solar system.
3 ____ Biography	**C.** An orphan from England settles in Australia at the start of the nineteenth century.
4 ____ Science Fiction	**D.** I was born in an old log cabin in 1878.
5 ____ Autobiography	**E.** Homework, homework I hate you, you stink. I hate you because you make me think.
6 ____ Fantasy	**F.** Three kids build a time machine out of an old car and a computer, and visit the future.
7 ____ Realistic Fiction	**G.** Once upon a time there was a little girl.
8 ____ Fairy Tales	**H.** He was as big as an ox.
9 ____ Tall Tales	**I.** Sarah misses her father. Her parents got divorced last year.
10 ____ Nonfiction	**J.** He created the name Dr. Seuss in 1937 with the publication of his first book, *And to Think I Saw It on Mulberry Street.*

Student Reading Profile

Name _____ Grade _____

School Year _____

Titles/Author(s)	Date Started	Date Completed	Genre

Genre Study Record Keeper

Year _____

Biography/Autobiography

Fairy Tales

Name

Name	Characteristics Web	Events Catalog	Picture Map	Role Models	Time Line Organizer	You and Me	Interview Organizer			Letter to a Character	Fairy Tale Comparison Chart	Fairy Tale Lesson	Heroes and Villains	Popularity Graph	Wanted Poster	Newspaper Article		

Genre Study Record Keeper

Year _____

Fantasy

Historical Fiction

Name

	Identifying Story Elements	Types of Fantasy	Problem & Solution	Illustrate a Character	What Happened When?	Character Paragraphs	Fantasy Elements Around Us			Character Map	Could This Be True?	The Life and Times of. . .	Who, What, When, Where, Why, How?	Extra! Extra!	Notes About a Main Character	Epitaph		

Genre Study Record Keeper

Year _____

Nonfiction   **Poetry**

Name	Text Features	Nonfiction Versus Fiction	What's It All About?	Question the Topic	KWL	Table of Facts	Captions				Feeling Poems	Haiku	Alliteration Adventure	Write Your Own Poem	Letter to a Poet	Poet's Style	Shape Poems		

Genre Study Record Keeper

Year _____

Realistic Fiction

Science Fiction

Name

	Perspectives	Story Steps	Telegram	Decisions, Decisions, Decisions	Obstacles	Lights, Camera, Action!	Get a Job			Time Capsule	Character Traits	Making Connections	One Hundred Years From Now	Science Fiction Story Elements	Types of Science Fiction	Same Problem, Different Solution		

Genre Study Record Keeper

Year _____

Tall Tales

Name	Exaggerations	Illustrate a Simile	Real or Superhuman Character Traits	Hero/Heroine?	Writing Your Own Tall Tale	Acrostic Poem	Guess Who?			Notes

Biography/Autobiography

Books for Modeling

Adler, David. *A Picture Book of Benjamin Franklin*. (Holiday, 1990).

Brenner, Martha. *Abe Lincoln's Hat*. (Random House, 1994).

Fritz, Jean. *Will You Sign Here, John Hancock?* (Putnam and Grosset Group, 1997).

Lundell, Margo. *A Girl Named Helen Keller*. (Scholastic, 1995).

Sullivan, George. *Quarterbacks! Eighteen of Football's Greatest*. (Atheneum Books for Young Readers, 1998).

Primary Books

Adler, David. *A Picture Book of Thomas Jefferson*. (Holiday, 1990).

Adler, David. *Dr. Martin Luther King, Jr.* (Holiday House, 2001).

Coles, Robert. *The Story of Ruby Bridges*. (Scholastic, 1995).

Cooney, Barbara. *Eleanor*. (Viking, 1996).

Freedman, Russell. *The Life and Death of Crazy Horse*. (Holiday House, 1996).

Freedman, Russell. *Out of Darkness: The Story of Louis Braille*. (Clarion Books, 1999).

Fritz, Jean. *Who's That Stepping on Plymouth Rock?* (PaperStar Books, 1998).

Kellogg, Steven. *Johnny Appleseed*. (Morrow Junior Books, 1988).

Wallner, Alexandra. *Laura Ingalls Wilder*. (Holiday House, 1997).

Intermediate Books

Adler, David. *Jackie Robinson: He Was the First*. (Holiday, 1989).

Dahl, Roald. *Boy: Tales of Childhood*. (Farrar, Straus & Giroux, 1984).

Ferris, Jeri. *Go Free or Die: A Story About Harriet Tubman*. (Carolrhoda, 1989).

Fritz, Jean. *And Then What Happened Paul Revere?* (PaperStar Books, 1996).

Greenberg, Keith Elliot. *Magic Johnson: Champion With a Cause*. (Lerner, Greene, Bette, 1992).

McGovern, Ann. *The Secret Soldier: The Story of Deborah Sampson*. (Scholastic, 1990).

Peet, Bill. *Bill Peet: An Autobiography*. (Houghton, 1994).

Sullivan, George. *Pitchers: Twenty-Seven of Baseball's Greatest*. (Aladdin Paperbacks, 1999).

Tackach, Jim. *Hank Aaron*. (Chelsea, 1991).

Fairy Tales

Books for Modeling

Galdone, Paul. *Jack and the Beanstalk*. (Clarion, 1982).

Hyman, Trina Schart. *Little Red Riding Hood*. (Holiday House, 1986).

Munsch, Robert. *The Paper Bag Princess*. (Annick Press, 1988).

Primary Books

Cole, Babette. *Princess Smartypants.* (Putnam, 1987).

Galdone, Paul. *Rumpelstiltskin.* (Clarion, 1990).

Goode, Diane. *Cinderella the Dog and Her Little Glass Slipper.* (Blue Sky Press, 2000).

Kimmel, Eric. *The Runaway Tortilla.* (Winslow Press, 2000).

Scieszka, Jon. *The Frog Prince Continued.* (Viking, 1991).

Scieszka, Jon. *The True Story of the Three Little Pigs.* (Viking, 1989).

Sturges, Philemon. *The Little Red Hen Makes a Pizza.* (Dutton Children's Books, 1999).

Intermediate Books

Climo, Shirley. *The Egyptian Cinderella.* (HarperCollins, 1992).

Donoghue, Emma. *Kissing the Witch: Old Tales in New Skins.* (HarperCollins, 1999).

Jackson, Ellen. *Cinder Edna.* (Lothrop, 1994).

Levine, Gail Carson. *The Fairy's Mistake.* (HarperCollins, 1999).

Martin, Rafe. *The Rough-Face Girl.* (PaperStar Books).

Stieg, Jeanne. *A Handful of Beans.* (HarperCollins, 1998).

Yolen, Jane. *King Long Shanks.* (Hartcourt Brace, 1998).

Young, Ed. *LonPoPo: A Red-Riding Hood Story From China.* (Philomel, 1989).

Fantasy

Books for Modeling

Andersen, Hans Christian. *The Princess and the Pea.* (Holiday House, 1988).

Van Allsburg, Chris. *Jumanji.* (Houghton Mifflin, 1981).

White, E.B. *Charlotte's Web.* (HarperCollins, 1952).

Wood, Audrey. *Heckedy Peg.* (Hartcourt Brace Jovanovich, 1987).

Yolen, Jane. *Child of Faerie, Child of Earth.* (Little, Brown & Company, 2001).

Primary Books

dePaola, Tomie. *Strega Nona.* (Simon & Schuster, 1997).

Freeman, Don. *Corduroy.* (Viking Penguin, 1985).

Lester, Helen. *Me First.* (Houghton Mifflin, 1992).

Lobel, Arnold. *Frog and Toad Are Friends.* (HarperCollins, 1979).

Peterson, John. *The Littles.* (Scholastic, 1993).

Polacco, Patricia. *Appelemando's Dreams.* (PaperStar Books, 1997).

Sadler, Marilyn. *Alistair Underwater.* (Simon & Schuster, 1990).

Steig, William. *Sylvester and the Magic Pebble.* (Aladdin Publishers, 1973).
Van Allsburg, Chris. *Bad Day at Riverbend.* (Houghton Mifflin, 1995).
Wood, Audrey. *The Flying Dragon Room.* (Scholastic, 2000).

Intermediate Books

Banks, Lynne Reid. *The Indian in the Cupboard.* (Avon, 1988).
Catling, Patrick Skene. *The Chocolate Touch.* (William Morrow, 1979).
Cleary, Beverly. *The Mouse and the Motorcycle.* (William Morrow, 1989).
Dahl, Roald. *James and the Giant Peach.* (Puffin Books, 2001).
Dahl, Roald. *Matilda.* (Puffin Books, 1990).
King-Smith, Dick. *Babe: The Gallant Pig.* (Crown, 1993).
Lewis, C.S. *The Lion, the Witch, and the Wardrobe.* (HarperCollins, 1994).
Rowling, J.K. *Harry Potter and the Sorcerer's Stone.* (Scholastic, 2001).
Titus, Eve. *Basil and the Lost Colony.* (Minstrel, 1989).

Historical Fiction

Books for Modeling

Bunting, Eve. *Dandelions.* (Voyager Books, 2001).
Houston, Gloria. *My Great-Aunt Arizona.* ((HarperCollins, 1992).
Sandin, Joan. *The Long Way to a New Land.* (HarperCollins, 1986).

Primary Books

Cohen Barbara. *Molly's Pilgrim.* (Lothrop, 1998).
Johnston, Tony. *The Quilt Story.* (PaperStar Books, 1996).
MacLachlan, Patricia. *Sarah, Plain and Tall.* (HarperCollins 1987).
McLerran, Alice. *Roxaboxen.* (Lothrop, 1991).
Rylant, Cynthia. *When I Was Young in the Mountains.* (Dutton, 1992).

Intermediate Books

Bunting, Eve. *The Train to Somewhere.* (Clarion Books, 2000).
Bunting, Eve. *The Wall.* (Clarion, 1990).
Hall, Donald. *Ox-Cart Man.* (Viking, Puffin, 1983).
Lowry, Lois. *Number the Stars.* (Laurel Leaf Library, 1998).
Polacco, Patricia. *Pink and Say.* (Philomel, 1994).
Wilder, Laura Ingalls. *Little House on the Prairie* series. (HarperCollins, 1987).

Nonfiction

Books for Modeling

Lepthien, Emilie. *Wolves* (A New True Book). (Children's Press, 1991).

Masoff, Joy. *Oh, Yuck! The Encyclopedia of Everything Nasty.* (Workman Publishing, 2000).

Patent, Dorothy Hinshaw. *Bold and Bright, Black-and-White Animals.* (Walker & Company, 1998).

Simon, Seymour. *Wolves.* (HarperCollins, 1995).

Tanaka, Shelley. *The Buried City of Pompeii.* (Hyperion, 1997).

Primary Books

Crewe, Sabrina. *The Mountain Lion* (Life Cycles series). (Raintree/Steck-Vaughn, 1998).

Gans, Roma. *Let's Go Rock Collecting* (Let's Read and Find Out Science series). (HarperCollins, 1997).

Kallen, Stuart A. *The Police Station* (Field Trip series). (ABDO & Daughters, 1997).

Kunhardt, Edith. *Pompeii . . . Buried Alive!* (Random House, 1987).

Liebman, Dan. *I Want to Be a Police Officer.* (Firefly Books, 2000).

Ready, Dee. *Police Officers* (Community Helpers series). (Bridgestone Books, 1997).

Saunders-Smith, Gail. *Lightning* (Weather series). (Capstone Press, 1998).

Intermediate Books

Cole, Joanna. *The Magic School Bus* series. (Econo-Clad Books, 1999).

Hemstock, Annie. *The Moose.* (Capstone High/Low Books, 1999).

Martin, Patricia A. Fink. *Gorillas* (A True Book). (Children's Press, 2000).

Patent, Dorothy Hinshaw. *Polar Bears* (Carolrhoda Nature Watch Book). (Carolrhoda Books, 2000).

Perry, Phyllis. *Freshwater Giants* (Watts Library-series). (Franklin Watts, 2000).

Simon, Seymour. *Gorillas.* (HarperCollins, 2000).

Swanson, Diane. *Animals Eat the Weirdest Things.* (Henry Holt & Company, 1998).

Wexo, John Bonnett. *Wolves.* (Wildlife Ed., Ltd., 1986).

Poetry

Books for Modeling

Fleischman, Paul. *Joyful Noise: Poems for Two Voices.* (HarperCollins, 1992).

Graham, Joan Bransfield. *Flicker Flash.* (Houghton Mifflin, 1999).

Graves, Donald. *Baseball, Snakes, and Summer Squash: Poems About Growing Up.* (Boyds Mill Press, 1996).

Moss, Jeffrey. *Butterfly Jar.* (Bantam, 1989).

Routman, Regie. *Kids' Poems.* (Scholastic, 2000).

Primary Books

Grossman, Bill. *Timothy Tunny Swallowed a Bunny.* (Laura Geringer Book, 2001).

Lalli, Judy. *I Like Being Me: Poems for Children About Feeling Special, Appreciating Others, and Getting Along.* (Free Spirit Publishing, 1997).

Lansky, Bruce. *Miles of Smiles: Kids Pick the Funniest Poems.* (Meadowbrook Press, 1998).

Lewis, J. Patrick. *Doodle Dandies: Poems That Take Shape.* (Simon & Schuster, 1998).

Otten, Charlotte F. *January Rides the Wind: A Book of Months.* (HarperCollins, 1997).

Weil, Zaro. *Mud, Moon, and Me.* (Houghton Mifflin, 1992).

Intermediate Books

Fleischman, Paul. *Big Talk: Poems for Four Voices.* (Candlewick Press, 2000).

Greenfield, Eloise. *Night on Neighborhood Street.* (Dial, 1991).

Kennedy, X.J. and Dorothy M. Kennedy. *Knock at a Star: A Child's Introduction to Poetry.* (Little, Brown. 1999).

McNaughton, Colin. *Wish You Were Here (and I Wasn't): A Book of Poems and Pictures for Globe Trotters.* (Candlewick Press, 2000).

Prelutsky, Jack. *It's Raining Pigs and Noodles.* (Greenwillow Books, 2000).

Prelutsky, Jack (editor). *The 20th Century Children's Poetry Treasury.* (Alfred A. Knopf, 1999).

Shields, Carol Diggory. *Lunch Money and Other Poems About School.* (Dutton, 1995).

Silverstein, Shel. *Where the Sidewalk Ends.* (HarperCollins, 1974).

Professional Resources

Bauer, Caroline Feller. *The Poetry Break.* (H.W. Wilson, 2000).

Realistic Fiction

Books for Modeling

Bunting, Eve. *Fly Away Home.* (Clarion, 1993).

Gaiman, Neil. *The Day I Swapped My Dad for Two Goldfish.* (White Wolf, 1998).

Lorbiecki, Marybeth. *Just One Flick of a Finger.* (Dial, 1996).

MacLachlan, Patricia. *All the Places to Love.* (HarperCollins, 2000).

Viorst, Judith. *Alexander and the Terrible, Horrible, No Good, Very Bad Day.* (Atheneum Books, 1972).

Primary Books

Blaine, Marge. *The Terrible Thing That Happened at My House.* (Four Winds, 1984).

Fox, Mem. *Wilfrid Gordon McDonald Partridge.* (Kame/Miller, 1995).

Giff, Patricia Reilly. *The Candy Corn Contest.* (Econo-Clad Books, 1999).

Herron, Carolivia. *Nappy Hair.* (Knopf, 1997).

Henkes, Kevin. *Lilly's Purple Plastic Purse.* (Greenwillow, 1996).

Krisher, Trudy. *Kathy's Hats: A Story of Hope.* (Albert Whitman and Company, 1992).

Rockwell, Thomas. *How to Eat Fried Worms.* (Dell, 1989).

Viorst, Judith. Alexander, *Who's Not (Do you hear me? I mean it!) Going to Move.*
    (Aladdin Paperbacks, 1998).

Williams, Vera B. *A Chair for My Mother.* (Greenwillow Books, 1987).

Intermediate Books

Armstrong, William. *Sounder.* (HarperCollins, 1969).

Cleary, Beverly. *Dear Mr. Henshaw.* (Avon, 2000).

Cleary, Beverly. *Ramona Quimby, Age 8.* (Avon, 1992).

Danziger, Paula. *Amber Brown Wants Extra Credit.* (Little Apple, 1997).

Johnson, Dolores. *Papa's Stories.* (MacMillan, 1994.)

McSwigan, Marie. *Snow Treasure.* (Scholastic, 1988).

Naylor, Phyllis Reynolds. *Shiloh.* (Aladdin Paperbacks, 2000).

Paterson, Katherine. *Bridge to Terabithia.* (HarperCollins, 1987).

Paulsen, Gary. *Brian's Winter.* (Laurel Leaf Library, 1998).

Peterson, John. *The Littles.* (Little Apple Books, 1993).

Science Fiction

Books for Modeling

Diterlizzi, Tony. *Jimmy Zangwow's Out-of-this-World Moon Pie Adventure.*
    (Simon & Schuster, 2000).

Peet, Bill. *The Wump World.* (Houghton Mifflin, 1974).

Pinkwater, Daniel. *Wallpaper From Space.* (Atheneum Books, 1996).

Slote, Alfred. *My Robot Buddy.* (HarperCollins, 1986).

Walsh, Jill Paton. *The Green Book.* (Sunburst, 1986).

Primary Books

Kirk, David. *Nova's Ark.* (Scholastic, 1999).

Marshall, Edward. *Space Case.* (Dial, 1986).

Rosen, Michael. *Mission Ziffoid.* (Candlewick Press, 1999).

Sadler, Marilyn. *Alistair's Time Machine.* (Aladdin, 1989).

Sadler, Marilyn. *Zenon: Girl of the 21st Century.* (Simon & Schuster, 1996).

Yolen, Jane. *Commander Toad and the Big Black Hole.* (Econo-Clad, 1999).

Yolen, Jane. *Commander Toad in Space.* (PaperStar Books, 1996).

Intermediate Books

Asimov, Janet. *Norby and the Terrified Taxi.* (Walker and Company, 1997).

Brennan, Herbie. *The Mystery Machine.* (Margaret K. McElderry, 1995).

Coville, Bruce. *My Teacher Fried My Brains.* (Minstrel, 1991).

Etra, Jonathan & Spinner, Stephanie. *Aliens for Lunch.* (Random House, 1991).

Gutman, Dan. *Virtually Perfect.* (Hyperion Books for Children, 1998).

Pinkwater, Daniel. *Borgel.* (Aladdin, 1992).

Pinkwater, Daniel. *Ned Feldman, Space Pirate.* (MacMillan, 1994).

Service, Pamela. *Stinker From Space.* (Scribner, 1988).

Slote, Alfred. *Omega Station.* (Lippincott Williams, 1983).

Spinner, Stephanie & Bisson, Terry. *Be First in the Universe.* (Yearling, 2001).

Tall Tales

Books for Modeling

Blair, Walter. *Tall Tale America: A Legendary History of Our Humorous Heroes.* (University of Chicago Press, 1987).

Osborne, Mary Pope. *American Tall Tales.* (Knopf, 1991).

San Souci, Robert D. *Larger Than Life: The Adventures of American Legendary Heroes.* (Bantam Doubleday Dell, 1995).

Stoutenburg, Adrien. *American Tall Tales.* (Penguin, 1976).

Primary Books

Aliki. *The Story of Johnny Appleseed.* (Aladdin, 1987).

Dewey, Ariane. *Febold Feboldson.* (Greenwillow, 1984).

Kellogg, Steven. *Mike Fink.* (Mulberry Books, 1998).

Kellogg, Steven. *Paul Bunyan.* (William Morrow, 1985).

Kellogg, Steven. *Pecos Bill.* (Mulberry Books, 1992).

Ketteman, Helen. *Luck With Potatoes.* (Orchard Books, 1995).

Stoutenburg, Adrien. *American Tall Tales.* (Penguin, 1976).

Intermediate Books

Gleiter, Jan. *Paul Bunyan and Babe the Blue Ox.* (Raintree, 1995).

Kellogg, Steven. *I Was Born About 10,000 Years Ago.* (Mulberry Books, 1988).

Lyman, Nanci A. *Paul Bunyan.* (Troll Communications, 1980).

Lyman, Nanci A. *Pecos Bill.* (Troll Communications, 1980).

Rounds, Glen. *The Morning the Sun Refused to Rise: An Original Paul Bunyan Tale.*
   (Holiday, 1984).

Sanfield, Steve. *A Natural Man: The True Story of John Henry.* (David R. Godine, 1990).

Wood, Audrey. *The Bunyans.* (Blue Sky Press, 1996).

Notes